Creation

Creation

A Theology for the Here and Now, Volume Two

ANDY ROSS

RESOURCE *Publications* · Eugene, Oregon

CREATION
A Theology for the Here and Now, Volume Two

Copyright © 2022 Andy Ross. All rights reserved. Except for brief quotations in critical publications or reviews, no part of this book may be reproduced in any manner without prior written permission from the publisher. Write: Permissions, Wipf and Stock Publishers, 199 W. 8th Ave., Suite 3, Eugene, OR 97401.

Resource Publications
An Imprint of Wipf and Stock Publishers
199 W. 8th Ave., Suite 3
Eugene, OR 97401

www.wipfandstock.com

PAPERBACK ISBN: 978-1-6667-4509-2
HARDCOVER ISBN: 978-1-6667-4510-8
EBOOK ISBN: 978-1-6667-4511-5

JULY 11, 2022 10:09 AM

Scripture texts in this work are taken from the New American Bible, revised edition © 2010, 1991, 1986, 1970 Confraternity of Christian Doctrine, Washington, D.C. and are used by permission of the copyright owner. All Rights Reserved. No part of the New American Bible may be reproduced in any form without permission in writing from the copyright owner.

To Rebecca

Split a piece of wood; I am there.
Lift up a stone, and you will find me there.

—*The Gospel of Thomas*[1]

---

1. Meyer, *Thomas*, 20.

Contents

On Words: A Prologue to Creation	1
Beginnings	6
God's Desire	18
Expansion and Complexification	29
Self-Actualization	43
In the End	56
On Practice: An Epilogue to Creation	62
Bibliography	65

On Words
A Prologue to Creation

What cannot be spoken with words, but that whereby words are spoken: Know that alone to be Brahman.

—KENA UPANISHAD[1]

WE CANNOT NOT COMMUNICATE. Even if I choose to say nothing, I am still communicating something. Communication is how we express ourselves. It is how we share our experience of life with others. And, yet, the journey from experience to thought to word is limiting. Though language is beautiful, it can never quite grasp the nuance of even the simplest experience.

The process of language is this: we experience life; we conceptualize that experience; we express that conceptualization. I walk out of my house in the morning and see the sun peaking over the trees. I think to myself, "this is beautiful." When I get to work, I try and describe the sunrise to a coworker. "I walked out of my house and the sky was

1. Mascaro, *Upanishads*, 51.

illuminated by the soft glow of morning rays—pink, purple, and blue." I experience a sunrise, I consider the experience, and I communicate the experience. This is communication.[2]

Understanding, or conceptualizing, our experiences is an ongoing process. As I experience life, my storehouse of knowledge grows, and as knowledge grows, so does understanding. But a thought cannot contain even the simplest experience. I think I know what it is to touch these keys, but my thoughts are a shadow of the experience of fingers touching keyboard. The conceptualization of an experience is not the experience. How could it be? A thought is a thought, and an experience is an experience.[3] During the process, something is always lost.

Language is the process of expressing thought. The paragraphs I write, the words I say, and the plethora of other ways I express myself are my attempts at communicating what I am thinking about a specific subject at a specific moment. And just as thoughts cannot contain experience, words cannot contain thought. Thoughts are tangled and abstract; words tend to be solid and stoic. In my desire to be understood and to understand, I speak and I listen. But what is communicated is not what is thought, and what is thought is not what is experienced. Something is always lost in translation.

POINTS OF REFERENCE

Language is as beautiful as it is messy, and though language is limited, its value cannot be overstated. The cultures of the world and the religious traditions that spring from these

---

2. Communication is not limited to words. We communicate with body language, sound, silence, etc.

3. It should be noted here that we also experience thoughts.

cultures are made possible by our ability to communicate. The more we are able to share our experiences, the better we are able to participate in the wonder of creation. All I have is my experience of life until I communicate. It is through the miracle of language that I am invited to realities beyond my own. The reality of God is no exception.

Language can never fully describe the experience of life. Even tangible realities experienced through the senses cannot be grasped by words. And, yet, tangible realities have a point of reference to help facilitate understanding. As I describe the sunrise to my coworker, I am relying on the assumption that she has seen a sunrise before. And, if she has not seen a sunrise before (however unlikely), she does have at least some rudimentary experience of the sun and the colors pink, purple, and blue.

No matter how different our circumstances, all humans share the basic experience of life. Thus, we a have common ground through which communication can be established. This communication can be difficult, but it is always possible. We know what it is to breathe, to eat, to sleep, to get angry, to forgive—we are more alike than we are different, and this commonality is the bedrock of communication. I am sitting in a chair, drinking coffee, and typing on a computer. If I had a desire to communicate this experience, I could assume that at least some of what I am doing would translate. The experience itself would not and could not, but there is, at least, a commonality to the objects of my experience.

When we seek to communicate the experience of God, there is an added layer of difficulty. The reality of God is intangible. God is not something that we can touch, taste, hear, smell, or see. We experience God through creation, but the experience itself transcends the physical and energetic world. The process, however, is the same. We experience God, we conceptualize the experience, and we seek to communicate the experience to others. What we must rely on is a language specifically suited to spirituality.

RELIGIOUS LANGUAGE

There are some who claim that religious language is metaphorical. This is true in a certain sense. Metaphorical language applies certain characteristics of a word or phrase to something else in order to describe an aspect of its nature. If I told you that my wife was a bee, you might assume that she works tirelessly. Your assessment would be based on the "bee" as a point of reference. Many understand bees to be hard workers, and you could rightly deduce that this is the very characteristic that I am applying to my wife. Of course, the metaphor is based upon the assumption that you share this understanding of bee-hood. The best metaphors are those that utilize points of reference that are commonly understood by the intended audience.[4]

Religious language works in a similar manner. In conceptualizing the experience of God, images are revealed to us that reflect aspects of God's nature. In fact, this process is often referred to as revelation. Because creation is an expression of God, the reality of God can be revealed to us at any moment. When this happens, our minds seek to conceptualize the experience through reflective imagery. The experience of God is wrapped in thought so that it may be engaged, deepened, and communicated.

The word "spirituality" comes from the Latin *spiritus*, which means breath. Breath as a religious image is used

---

4. Some metaphors work on the opposite premise, utilizing points of reference that challenge assumptions.

in a myriad of religious traditions as a description of our experience of God. All humans know what it is to breathe, whether or not we have reflected on the experience. Therefore, breath as a religious image has almost universal significance. We exist through constant participation with the world around us. We take in oxygen and release carbon dioxide. It is the constant replenishing of breath that sustains us. Breath is within us, and breath is around us.

Our experience of God resonates deeply with our experience of breathing. We experience God as within and beyond us, as that which sustains our existence. God is not oxygen; God is not breathing.[5] Breath is merely an image. The image works if it activates the reference point—God itself. Religious language points to the experience of God and arises directly from that experience. Just as God is revealed in creation, God is revealed in our religious language. And, in the process, new revelations are born.

THE TEXT

This book you are reading now (and I am glad you are!) is the second in a series of theological texts grounded in my experience of God. While the first was an introduction and my attempt to catalyze my theology through the writing process, this book is dedicated to creation. Why does God create? How does God create? Why should we care? You may find that you share many of my thoughts on God and creation; you may not. Either way, remember—these are just words. What matters most is how God is revealed to you, even if you never use that "word."

---

5. Though, in actuality, God is all things.

Beginnings

Time isn't precious at all, because it is an illusion. What you perceive as precious is not time but the one point that is out of time: the Now.

—ECKHART TOLLE[1]

EVERY STORY HAS A BEGINNING. According to scientific consensus, the physical universe began over 13 billion years ago with a "big bang." In comparison, I was born a mere 40 years ago. Life is a hierarchy of forms[2] rising and falling. The birth of any form signifies its arrival on a plane of existence, the moment it becomes present within the horizon of creation.

We typically think of birth in terms of physical forms. If we are discussing the birth of a child, we may point to the moment of conception. A sperm and an egg, each having already come into form, meet and a new life commences. Or we may choose a different point of departure, perhaps

1. Tolle, *Power of Now*, 49.

2. The term "form" is used to signify any object within creation. All created objects come into being in the form of something, whether a physical form (tree, star, atom) or subtle form (thought).

when the fetus becomes viable or when the baby is born 40 weeks after conception. But whatever criteria we use, the birth of a child signifies the moment it comes into being as a unique form within creation.

When we consider the birth, or beginning, of other physical forms, the question is the same: at what point did this form arrive as a distinguishable entity within the hierarchy? Stars, planets, fish, amoeba, and all other physical forms come into existence and inevitably go out, including the universe itself. If we picture physical reality as a hierarchy of physical forms rising and falling, then the universe is simply the outer edge of the hierarchy. As each form within the hierarchy has a beginning, so does the hierarchy itself. Of course, the universe may simply be a part of an even larger, more complex hierarchy, but that has yet to be observed.

Birth as a concept does not have to be isolated to physical phenomena. All forms have a beginning. The essence of being a created thing is that there is a moment of creation or "being created." Mental phenomena come in and out of form just like their physical counterparts. Each thought has a moment of arrival on the mental plane, a moment of birth. Though thoughts are subtle forms, meaning that they cannot be observed by the physical senses, they follow the same pattern of birth, life, and death.

We experience creation as a hierarchy of interrelated forms, physical and mental. These forms have a moment of creation and a moment of departure.[3] In fact, if we define a "moment" as the experience of a particular configuration of forms, a single freezeframe of the hierarchy, then we could say that each moment is born, and each moment dies. As

---

3. Death as the "moment of departure" will be discussed in the final chapter.

the forms that comprise the particularity of the moment change, so does the moment. The moment is born, the moment dies, and another moment takes its place.

All created things have a moment of creation; all stories have a beginning. We typically describe the beginning of creation as the big bang. If we are considering creation as the rise and fall of phenomena within the physical universe, then the big bang would be the most logical beginning to our story. We know of nothing beyond the physical universe. It is the horizon of our experience of physical reality. Following this line of reasoning, we would state unequivocally that creation began 13 billion years ago.

If this were a scientific text, this is where our story would begin. Science is, after all, the ongoing examination of physical reality, and physical reality as we know it began some 13 billion years ago. But this is not the story of creation; this is the story of *God and creation*. And our story must begin at the place where God and creation meet.

NO BEGINNING

Every form, the universe included, has a beginning. God, on the other hand, does not. Forms rise and fall; there is a moment of birth and, inevitably, a moment of death. God is not a form within creation. God is not a form beyond creation. God is not a form at all. Creation is a hierarchy of forms; God is the formless that gives rise to it all. This is our first and most important distinction between God and creation.

Distinctions between God and creation are problematic. Creation is an expression of God.[4] We can never

---

4. Panentheism is the belief that God is one with creation, yet creation does not exhaust what God is.

truly know where creation ends, and God begins. God is all, and all is God. And, yet, if we are to deepen our conscious relationship to God, we must endeavor to understand what God is in itself. One of the most pragmatic methods of accomplishing this task is through negation. If I know what creation is, and I do, I can subtract all that is "created," and I will be left with God as the presence within and beyond it.

One of the best descriptions of God that I have come across provides such an understanding. In the Hindu traditions, God, or *Brahmin*, is described as *satchitananda*. This term can be translated as being (*sat*), consciousness (*chit*), and joy (*ananda*).[5]

BEING (SAT)

All forms in creation are expressions of being (*sat*). I am a human being, meaning I am a human expression of being itself. We could, of course, use this terminology to describe any form in creation. A star is a "star being," a rooster is a "rooster being," and a thought is a "thought being." This is to say that each of these forms is a manifestation, or expression, of being itself. If I subtract the form, I will arrive at the formless beneath it. If I subtract everything that is human from my situation, I will be left with being itself.

Consider everything that makes you "human," and I do mean everything. You are a hierarchy of forms. Your physical body is a hierarchy of molecules which are expressions of energy. You experience this energy as sensations in the physical body and emotions in the energetic body (the body of energy that supports the physical body). These experiences and the experience of other forms surrounding

---

5. *Ananda* is one of the three spiritual states—peace, love, and joy—and will be discussed in a future text.

you are stored and given meaning within the mind. Over time the mind takes on the quality of personality or ego. Ego is the mind's self-reflected image, simply put, "who I think I am." The physical body and mind are expressions of life; they are hierarchies of form. They are expressions of being.

Everything that makes you a unique expression of being (*sat*), everything that makes you *you*, is a part of creation. Your physical body is a hierarchy of forms within a larger hierarchy of forms. And your mind, as a hierarchy of mental forms, has evolved to distinguish *you* as a unique and separate entity. All of creation is a temporal expression of God. While some contend that humans are endowed with an eternal, individual soul that is separate from God, this belief is actually a roadblock to understanding the relationship between God and creation.

Spirt and Soul

God is an eternal unified reality. God (*satchitananda*) has no beginning and no end; God just is. Creation is an expression of that reality. Though we cannot separate creation from God, theologically we consider the two as a primordial duality. There is God, the ground of being or being itself, then there is creation as an expression of being. God is the one eternal reality. Everything else is a temporal expression of that reality. The term "soul," as it is often used, misrepresents God's relationship to creation by positing the existence of individual eternal entities that are reliant on but separate from God itself. Our "soul" is not an individual spirit inhabiting the body. Soul is the place where spirit and body meet.

The term "spirit" is most often used to signify the experience of God within creation. God and spirit are synonymous. We experience the spirit of God, or God itself, within creation. This is, of course, natural since creation is quite literally an expression of God. The term "soul" is more nuanced. If spirit is the reality of God within creation, soul is where God and creation meet. Being becomes in the form of created things. Soul is the meeting place of being and form, the point of contact where God's being is emptied into creation. Spirit is one, but soul is unique to each expression.

The spirit of God is the animating presence beneath all forms. And, as each form is a unique expression of God's spirit, each expression bears a unique soul. All forms have soul. Soul is the movement of God within the form, the place where the eternal and temporal meet. We experience this relationship anywhere we find God expressed in life. Music is said to have soul when it moves us; food is said to have soul when it nourishes our entire being; people are said to have soul when their actions are in harmony with their creator. Spirit is one; soul is many. Soul connects us with God because soul is where God is met. Where we find soul, we find God.

Soul is best used when describing the intersection of eternity and temporality, being and form, spirit and matter. God is the only eternal reality. But God is eternally expressing itself as form; being (*sat*) is always becoming. Wipe away the totality of created things and you will be left with being itself. Yet there is a second distinct eternal property that can contribute to our limited understanding of God—consciousness (*chit*).

CONSCIOUSNESS (CHIT)

We experience reality as an expression of being (*sat*). We are surrounded by forms rising and falling on the physical and mental plane.[6] These forms are each a manifestation of being itself. There is one being (*sat*) which is eternally becoming. But have you ever considered where you experience reality *from*? If we are surrounded by a hierarchy of forms rising and falling, what is aware of them? I am aware of life; I am "conscious" of it. But what is consciousness? According to our description, *satchitananda*, God is consciousness. Or, more specifically, being is conscious.

Being (*sat*) is a term used to describe the formless ground that expresses itself in the myriad of forms that make up creation. Every form within the hierarchy is an expression of being. God is being, and being becomes in the creative act. Yet God is also consciousness (*chit*). The ground of existence, which is expressed in every form we encounter, is also conscious of all that it becomes. All of life is endowed with consciousness because being itself *is* conscious. Consciousness (*chit*) is the eye of God which experiences life. We are aware of life because God is aware of life. We view life from God's eternal presence. In fact, all of life does.

Mind

Consciousness is typically equated with the mind. The reason for this misidentification is that we equate the forms arising within consciousness with consciousness itself. What we call the "mind" is merely the hierarchy of forms

---

6. The energetic, physical, and mental planes will be revisited later in the text.

that make up our mental landscape. We experience life within two horizons: physical and mental. It is a mistake to equate existence itself with the forms that rise and fall within the horizon. All forms come and go, are born and die. Being itself cannot be reduced to what being becomes. And consciousness cannot be reduced to what it is conscious of.

We are constantly aware of forms rising and falling on the mental plane. This is not so different from our awareness of forms rising and falling on the physical plane. I am aware of physical forms through the five senses. As I move through creation, I am aware that my physical body is one form among many. I relate to the world around me; I interact with it. All that I know of physical creation, I know through the body. I change; creation changes. All forms come and go, and one day, my body will cease to be. Yet, while the countless expressions of being rise and fall, being remains. Being as an eternal reality never changes. It is not born; it does not die. Forms come and go; the formless simply is.

The mental plane is a hierarchy of thought forms rising and falling. These forms create a mental landscape that is as real to me as the physical landscape. Yet my experience of thought is different. I am conscious of both physical and mental forms. I am conscious of physical forms through the body. As I am typing these words, I am aware of the sensation of the keyboard beneath my fingers, the screen in front of my eyes, and the taste of coffee on my tongue. The physical forms that surround me are experienced via the body. I cannot, however, touch, see, or taste my thoughts. Mental forms are subtle expressions of being experienced on a purely mental plane.

The moment before I type, I consider the words that may best describe the subject at hand. Though I cannot see these thoughts, I am conscious of them. Thoughts are constantly rising and falling within my mind. Some of these I am consciously aware of, and some exist as the backdrop that comprises my conception of reality. If I could dissect the totality of my mental landscape (which is, by all accounts, impossible), I would find that it is similar to creation at large—a hierarchy of forms rising and falling within the eternal backdrop of being. This same backdrop is present within the mental sphere. It is being, experienced within us as consciousness.

Consciousness (*chit*) is not created by the mind. The mind is merely a hierarchy of forms arising within consciousness. Consciousness, like being, is singular. *Being is conscious.* This is difficult for us to fathom because we assume that we are conscious of life from the mind. The mind, however, is just another part of the hierarchy of creation. Thoughts rise and fall like all other forms. The mental landscape shifts and changes, but consciousness, like being, remains. We are conscious because being is conscious, because God is consciousness. Forms rise and fall as expressions of God's eternal being. God is conscious of those forms. And, therefore, so are we.

Subtract all expressions of being and you are left with being itself. Empty the mind of all thought, and you will be left with consciousness itself. *Satchitananda* is the formless within and beyond all form. We discover the presence of *satchitananda* in soulful, or soul-filled, moments. There are certain experiences that bring us face to face with God. A walk in the woods, a song on the radio, a conversation with an old friend, sitting silently in a temple—these and so many other experiences help us to discover the place where God and creation meet. In these moments we feel at one with life, like all that surrounds us emanates from the same presence. These are moments of spiritual truth. This is the beginning.

BEGINNING NOW

When does the story of God and creation begin? Where does it begin? All forms have a beginning; all forms are born. The formless has no beginning. God simply is. So where do God and creation meet? When is the moment of incarnation? The first lines in book of Genesis read, "In the beginning, when God created the heavens and the earth and the earth was without form or shape, with darkness over the abyss and a mighty wind sweeping over the waters—then God said: Let there be light, and there was light (1:1–3)."[7] This verse does not refer to the big bang. It refers to the eternal act of being becoming, the one moment from which all of life springs forth. Genesis is referring to now.

Time

We measure the rise and fall of temporal phenomenon (form) in time. While many consider time to be an existential aspect of creation, it is actually no more than a tool of measurement like inches or quarts. While space is an existential property of creation, the inch is part of a system derived to divide space into convenient increments. Time is the same. All forms change, they rise and fall, are born and die. Change is an existential property of creation. Time is how we measure change. It helps us to understand where we are within the hierarchy.

---

7. All biblical quotes from the *New American Bible Revised Edition*.

CREATION

Time utilizes the rotation of the earth on its axis (days), the orbit of the moon around the earth (months), and the orbit of the earth around the sun (years) as standards of measurement. These cycles are relatively consistent and therefore provide the necessary hash marks on the ruler of time. Since my birth, the earth has encircled the sun 40 times. In comparison, the universe is said to be 13 billion years old. Time helps us to make appointments, predict changes in the body and environment, learn from the past, and prepare for the future. Time is an essential component in our understanding of change. Beyond this understanding, however, it does not exist.

Life is change. As being becomes, life moves. We measure this movement in time. When I consider what was, I am considering a previous incarnation of the moment (a freezeframe of the hierarchy). When I consider what will be, I am speculating about one of the many possible incarnations of the moment that will grow out of this one. The hierarchy of creation continues to expand and contract as the forms within it are born, exist, and die. Being, however, remains, as does consciousness. Creation expands from God's eternal being and falls back into it. Previous incarnations of creation are a memory; future incarnations are an idea. God creates now.

Being is becoming in this moment, the one moment. Now is all there is. God cannot create yesterday and, subsequently, we cannot act tomorrow. This moment is all we have. Everything that you have ever done and all that you will ever do, you will do now. In order to test this theory, you can conduct a simple experiment. At any moment of any day of any week of any year, ask yourself, "is it now?" You will always come up with the same answer: "YES!" This is due to the truth that now is all that exists. Forms rise and fall around your awareness of them. Being becomes form; forms change, but being remains. Being is conscious of the forms that change, but consciousness remains. One being, one consciousness, one moment. Welcome to eternity.

The story of God and creation begins at the moment when being becomes, at the place where the formless and form meet. The moment is now, and the place is here. Wherever you are, whenever you believe it to be, this is the beginning. God is emptying itself into creation in this very moment. The story of God and creation is beginning now.

God's Desire

> *A spark of impenetrable darkness flashed within the concealed of the concealed, from the head of Infinity—a cluster of vapor forming in formlessness, thrust in a ring, not black, not white, not red, not green, no color at all.*
>
> —THE ZOHAR[1]

THE FORMLESS BECOMES FORM in the creative act. Being becomes and is conscious of all that is expressed. But why does God create? Why does being become? When we examine creation and all that arises within it, we wonder if there is a reason for it all. To know why God creates is to realize why we are here. Our purpose in life is intrinsically linked to God's purpose for creating life. To know God is to know meaning. And it all begins with experience.

---

1. Matt, *Zohar*, 107–108.

ONE EXPERIENCE

All that we know of life comes from our experience of it. Thoughts, emotions, memories, sense perceptions—all forms which arise within the mental and physical planes are encountered through the phenomenon of experience. Experience is the actuality of being becoming. When being becomes, it experiences becoming. This experience is the one experience that each and every form participates in. Every experience that we have is a variant of the singular experience of being alive. I am an expression of being; I am experiencing life. Through this experience of life, I encounter other expressions of being. Though the particularities of my experience are constantly changing, meaning the configuration of the hierarchy changes as the forms do, the root of the experience is one.

As I sit and look out of my window, I am conscious of many sensations. I see trees moving with the breeze and squirrels chasing one another. I smell the candles that are burning around me, and I witness the thoughts arising which interpret and ascribe meaning to it all. This is an experience of life, forms rising and falling around my awareness of them. My body and mind are part of the hierarchy of forms that comprise the particularity of the experience. I experience life through the body, yet the experience does not originate in the body. I interpret the experience within the mind, yet the experience does not originate within the mind. The experience originates in the source of life, in being becoming.

In order to better understand the singular experience of being alive, we can isolate my current experience to "I see a tree." If we unravel the hierarchy present within this sensation, we can state that "I am aware of the image produced by my mind from the light that is reflected off of this tree through my eyes." Even a seemingly one-dimensional experience like "seeing a tree" is actually the result of a complex hierarchy of forms interacting. The act of seeing involves forms which surround us (the tree itself is a hierarchy of forms), light, the various components of the eye, and a multitude of neurons. Every experience involves innumerable forms interacting. Yet every experience begins with "I am aware of," which is a variant of "I experience."

The root of experience is being becoming. All of life, in its numerous manifestations, is an expression of being. When being becomes, it is expressed as life. Being (*sat*) is also conscious (*chit*). If being becoming is the root of all experience, then consciousness (or awareness) is inexorably linked to it. To experience life is to be aware of life. As I experience the particularities of the moment, I am conscious of what I experience. You cannot have experience without awareness just as you cannot have being without consciousness. As we discuss the singularity of experience, it is important to note that experience and consciousness are two dimensions of the same phenomenon.

Reality as we know it is both singular and plural, one eternal being becoming all things (one eternal consciousness aware of all things). The act of seeing previously described is a singular experience comprising a multitude of forms. The forms are many; the experience is one. Though I am aware of many forms surrounding me, my awareness of them originates in consciousness. Sensations are transmitted through the body, forms are interpreted by the mind, but there is only one who is aware of this. At the center of life is God, being (*sat*) and consciousness (*chit*). God is having a single experience of life and is conscious of that experience. And we, as forms arising, participate in that experience.

SUBJECT / OBJECT

Every experience requires a subject to experience and an object or objects to be experienced. If I am looking at a tree, I am the subject witnessing the tree as an object. As we dissect the experience, the objects multiply, but the subject does not. "I am the subject who is witnessing the image produced by my mind from the light that is reflected off of this tree through my eyes." Stating that "I experience" or "I am aware of" is the same as stating "I am the subject who experiences / is aware of." "I" am always the subject of my experience. This is not a revelation. But understanding who "I am" is.

I am the single subject who experiences the many objects which surround me, the forms rising and falling around my awareness of them. But who is the subject? We typically identify this subject as the body or mind. This is an illusion, supported by the presence of the body and mind in the majority of our experiences.[2] As human beings, we experience life through a human body and interpret this experience via a human mind. These are the tools of experience, however, and not the subject who experiences them. A simple meditative exercise may help to break this illusion.

Exercise

Close your eyes and take a deep breath.

Pay attention to your body. Wiggle your toes, move your arms, and roll your neck. Now speak: "This is my body through which I experience life." As you continue to sit, consider your

---

2. Dreams are experienced within the mind but seemingly outside of the body, while meditative and other spiritual states are often experienced beyond both the body and mind.

connection to this body. It has shifted and changed during your life, but your connection to it has remained constant. How? What is it that has remained constant? What is it that has NOT changed? Return to your body, but this time speak as you move it: "I am wiggling my toes; I am moving my arms, I am rolling my neck." Who is this I? Your body has changed, but the I has not.

"I am not my body; I am the one experiencing my body."

Take another deep breath.

Pay attention to your thoughts. What are the mental forms that rise and fall within your mind? Now speak: "This is my mind through which I experience life." Consider your connection to this mind, to these thoughts. Are you who you "think" you are? Thoughts come and go, personality shifts, but your connection to the mind remains. How? What is it that has remained constant? What is it that has not changed? Return to your thoughts and speak: "I am the one who is thinking these thoughts. I am the one who is aware of this image of myself."

"My body changes; my thoughts shift; I do not."

"Who am I?"

This exercise is meant to make a distinction between subject and object. You are the subject who experiences the numerous objects which surround you. Your body and mind are not the source of your experience of life. They are not the subjects. They are merely part of the hierarchy of forms which make each experience unique. I am experiencing a particular configuration of forms which constitute a unique moment. My body and mind are a part of that configuration. I receive sense perceptions through the five senses and interpret these perceptions in the mind. The body and mind are the two constants that we carry with us through the experience of being alive.[3] They are not, however, the subject.

I experience my body, I experience my mind, and I experience phenomena beyond my body and mind. "I" am the subject. I am a human being, meaning, I (the subject) experience life as a human expression of being itself. Being becomes in the creative act. Being becoming is the root of experience. Therefore, when I experience life, I am experiencing being becoming. Being is also conscious. When being becomes, it is conscious of what it becomes. Being and consciousness are one. Being experiences life (becoming) and is conscious of it. I experience life and am conscious of it. I am being. I am consciousness. God is the subject. God is the I.

In the *Torah*, God reveals itself to Moses in the form of a burning bush. When Moses asks God's name, the reply is "I am that I am" (Hebrew: *ehyeh asher ehyeh*).[4] Though the wordplay is meant to be mysterious, there is an inherent significance to the name that continues to unfold as we engage it. The name refers to God as the origin of life, as the being that becomes all things. It refers to God as the ultimate subject. Every experience of life begins with "I am." Although we often misidentify this "I am" with our body or mind, the truth of creation is there is only one subject, only one "I"—God.

God is the subject who experiences the multitude of objects that make up the fabric of creation. Our individual experience of life is an expression of the one experience that is life. When I look at a tree, God looks at a tree. As I am typing these words, God is typing these words. Creation

---

3. The mind and body are relatively constant. At closer inspection, they are in constant flux.

4. Exodus 3:1–14

as we know it is a hierarchy of forms rising and falling on the physical and mental planes, a hierarchy of objects. There is, however, only a single subject. Being becomes all things; consciousness is conscious of all things. Being and consciousness are one. The one becomes the many in the creative act.

Every experience requires a subject to experience and an object, or objects, to be experienced. This relationship between subject and object is the primordial duality that makes creation possible. Without a subject there can be no experience; without an object there can be no experience; and, without this relationship, there can be no creation. God, the eternal subject, has no beginning and no end. God just is. Yet God as eternal subject cannot experience life. God in itself is a singularity, and experience requires duality.

GOD'S DESIRE

All forms in creation are driven by purpose. Purpose can be described as the reason that we are here, the reason that we are alive. Just as our experience of life is an expression of God's single experience of life, our purpose for being alive is an expression of God's single purpose for creating life. God as a single eternal subject cannot experience life. Experience requires the duality of subject / object. Thus, we discover in the eternal subject a single purpose or desire. Being is driven by the single desire to become; consciousness is driven by the single desire to be conscious *of*; God is driven by the single desire to create. God must realize itself. This is the purpose of creation: one divine reality seeking to know itself, to express itself as life. God cannot simply be; God must become.

How does duality arise from singularity? How does one eternal subject create an entire universe of objects? How does the one become many? God as a unified reality can only be; it cannot become. In order to become, God must realize itself as both subject and object. God must divide. In Kabbalah, this division is known as the divine contraction (Hebrew: *tzimtzum*). Imagine you are the one divine subject, referred to in Kabbalah as the endless one (*Ein Sof*). You are pure being and consciousness. You simply exist with nothing to be aware of.[5] What would be your only impulse? What would be the single drive of absolute being? What would be the one question?

Who am I?

This single drive, this one purpose, causes God to contract, turn in on itself, and divide. In this moment, God becomes both subject and object, and creation is born. But when God-the-subject witnesses God-the-object, what exactly does God witness? Being itself cannot be known; it has no qualities or attributes. It simply is. God must experience itself as something other than being. In order for God to know itself, being must become. Thus, in the single moment of creation, God moves. God witnessing God creates a vibration wherein being is expressed as the only reality that can be experienced: form.

Form

If being is to be expressed, it must be expressed in the form of something. "Form" signifies that created things have qualities or attributes. Some forms, such as atoms, trees, and stars, have physical properties, while some have

---

5. Achieving this state of pure being is often the goal of spiritual exercise.

properties that cannot be measured or observed. Thoughts, for example, are subtle forms. Thoughts have specific qualities; they have specific attributes. If I sit here and think of my wife, many thoughts arise. Though you could measure these thoughts as neurons firing in my brain, you cannot measure the form that each thought takes. I could, however, describe these thoughts to you. I could relate to you their specific attributes in the hope that you might better understand who I imagine my wife to be. I could relate to you the "form" that my thoughts of her take.

Now try and imagine a created thing with no form. This created thing, this expression of being, has no qualities or attributes. It has no physical shape, no motion, no experiential quality whatsoever. This takes us right back to where we began, with being itself—no form, no expression, simply being. God creates so that God can experience itself. This is why being becomes. There is no experience without form; there is no experience without some set of qualities to define the experience. Being must become form. Consciousness must be conscious of form. When God creates, it creates form. These forms rise from being itself; they are expressions of it.[6]

THE UNMOVED MOVER

Life is movement. Every form in creation moves. From the smallest subatomic particle to the universe itself, creation is a hierarchy of forms shifting and changing. Aristotle referred to God as the "unmoved mover," a notion adopted by Thomas Aquinas in one of his proofs for God's existence.[7] The theory states that every form in creation moves

6. In Zen Buddhism, creation is often referred to as "forms rising."
7. See Thomas Aquinas' *Summa Theologica*.

because it is moved by something. Time can be seen as a chain linking the current hierarchy of forms to the forms responsible for their movement and so on and so forth. This chain cannot, however, extend back forever. There must be an "unmoved mover," an entity which is responsible for the first movement. According to Aquinas, this "unmoved mover" is God.

God has the one desire to create. Being is driven to become; consciousness is driven to be conscious of. Thus, God turns within and, in witnessing itself, becomes both subject and object. This witnessing is the impulse that sets creation in motion, the primordial movement. When God-the-subject witnesses itself, God-the-object moves (being becomes). This becoming is the vibration that Hindus refer to as AUM. AUM is an echo of the creative act, the single motion of being becoming which is taking place here and now. Just as being is eternally becoming, so too, AUM is eternally moving within each of us.

Every form in creation is a result of God's single desire to realize itself. God-the-subject witnesses God-the-object as stars, trees, you and me. Each of us is a fulfillment of the purpose of life: to allow God to experience itself. As I am experiencing this moment, an experience which includes body, mind, light, and trees, God is experiencing it through me. Being is becoming the forms which comprise the particularity of this moment, and consciousness is aware of what being becomes. The purpose of this moment is experience itself. Just as the hierarchy of forms which make up this moment will never be repeated, so too, God will never have another opportunity to experience it. There is purpose imbedded within each and every experience of life. Creation is a hierarchy of forms expanding and contracting so that God can know God.

CREATION

We find purpose and meaning in many different types of experience. Whether we gain fulfillment from creating art or find our calling in serving others, we are in a constant search for meaning. And, yet, if we simply stop and allow the miracle of the eternal moment to wash over us, we will find that we have been living our purpose from the very beginning. The purpose of creation is being fulfilled within every experience here and now. Each form is an expression of God's desire to create, and that desire is both expressed and fulfilled in the creative act. All that we have to do is witness it.

Expansion and Complexification

Someone who has come to know a single particle knows the whole universe.

—Dogen[1]

God has a single desire—to create. All of creation is the result of this desire. We move because life moves within us. The one movement created by God-the-subject witnessing God-the-object is vibrating within all things here and now. Just as each experience of life is an expression of the one experience of being alive, all movement is one movement. But how does God become an atom? How does God become a star? How does God's single desire result in this amazing universe we inhabit? As life moves, it expands. As life expands, it complexifies. The result—everything!

---

1. Nishijima & Cross, *Shobogenzo*, 89.

MOVEMENT AND CHANGE

In the beginning[2], when God turns within and divides, God witnesses itself, becoming both subject and object. This witnessing is the impulse for the creative act. As God-the-subject knows God-the-object, God-the-object moves so that it can be known. This movement is AUM, a vibration that expands outward as the impetus for life. All of life moves. To be alive is to be animated by being, and being becomes as God-the-object moves. God becoming (AUM) is the one movement that moves all things. The first verse of the Gospel of John reads, "In the beginning was the Word, and the Word was with God, and the Word was God." The Word is the active principle of creation, the vibration of God-the-object moving.[3] All created things are moved by AUM.

AUM is not a form that can be measured or observed. God as being (*sat*) is unmanifest; it has no qualities or attributes. Being is the formless that gives rise to form. AUM is God moving; AUM is the formless in motion. AUM is not an expression of being; it is being becoming. If being is the eternal noun, AUM is the eternal verb. If being has endless potential to become all things, AUM is the movement that actualizes this potential. Creation is being expressed as form. AUM is the becoming that makes each expression possible. Once God moves, being becomes, and creation is inevitable.

The eternal law of movement and change exists within AUM. Once *what is* moves, it must become *what will be*. *What will be* is *what is* plus the movement that changed it. When God moves as AUM, it must change; it must

---

2. Recall that the beginning is now.

3. God-the-subject is the passive principle, the silent witness that beholds the creative act.

become. Being is formless, without qualities or attributes. When being changes, it must change into something other than itself. When God moves, the formless becomes form; that which has no quality becomes that which has quality. Creation, the realm of created things, is the inevitable result of God moving.

When God moves, God changes, being becomes, and the formless is expressed as form. Form signifies that whatever God becomes will inevitably have qualities or attributes; the formless will take on the "form" of something. God creates so that God can experience itself. This is why God divides; this is why being becomes. There is no experience without form; there is no experience without some set of qualities to define the experience. Being must become form. Consciousness must be conscious of form. All forms, and creation as the totality of forms, arise from being itself; they are expressions of it.

Being is boundless, without boundaries or properties. This is why being must become and why the potential of being becoming is infinite. Being will inevitably express itself as all possibilities. Consciousness will inevitably be conscious of all possible forms. We exist within an ongoing evolution of being becoming all things. Each form is a unique expression within an endless sea of expressions. Our view of creation is vast, but it is nothing compared to the ineffable potentiality of what God has and will become. It is enough, however, that we appreciate the vastness of our individual altitude. It is enough that we recognize the miracle of creation as it presents itself in front of our eyes.

PLANES OF EXISTENCE

We experience life within four interrelated planes of existence: physical, energetic, spiritual, and mental.[4] A plane of existence is a realm of experiential phenomena determined by the forms that exist within it. Every form experiences life (though most are not self-aware) at a specific altitude or plane. The altitude is determined by the nature of the form and forms themselves. For example, physical forms experience other physical forms on a physical plane due to their physical properties. As human beings, we experience life via a physical body. We are physical beings existing on a physical plane.

The Physical Plane

The physical plane is the plane of physical phenomena. The largest physical form that we are aware of is the universe itself.[5] All physical forms within the universe, from molecules to stars, exist as a part of this physical hierarchy. Just as each human being is a hierarchy of atoms, molecules, compounds, etc., the universe is a hierarchy of innumerable physical forms (plants, animals, planets, stars, solar systems, etc.). We have yet to glimpse beyond the confines of the physical universe; however, the universe may be a part of a more immense physical structure. There was a time when we were not aware of subatomic particles, but they have always been present on the physical plane.

---

4. These are planes of *human* experience, meaning they are the planes that human beings are aware of.

5. We are aware of the universe, but, in reality, the universe is beyond our comprehension.

Expansion and Complexification

As human beings, human expressions of being itself, we experience life via the five senses. We taste, touch, hear, smell, and see the world around us. This is the reason that our physical awareness is limited to the physical plane. We are physical beings experiencing a physical reality. A plane of existence is defined by the forms within it. The physical plane is made up of physical forms; we interact on this plane via a physical body. We can only experience the levels of reality (the plane of existence) that we are a part of. Our experience of life is not just physical, however. We are a part of, and experience, other planes of existence.

The Energetic Plane

All physical forms, which make up an experiential hierarchy called the physical plane, are expressions of energy. We cannot taste, touch, hear, smell, or see energy, but we can, and do, experience the constant effects of energy (the expressions of it). Energy is actualized movement. Whereas AUM is the unmanifest movement of God (being becoming), energy is that movement actualized within our reality. The law of conservation of energy states that the energy within a system cannot be created nor can it be destroyed. When AUM breaks the plane of our reality, it becomes the energy of our system—creation.[6]

The physical plane is an expression of the energetic plane, just as all physical forms are expressions of energy. The energetic plane transcends and includes all physical phenomena.[7] All forms within creation are expressions of

---

6. Creation as we know it, i.e., the universe.

7. There is no existential divide between the energetic and physical plane. All of life is energy. We make this distinction in order to better understand our experience of creation.

energy, and energy is in constant motion. As energy moves, creation moves; and as creation moves, it changes. Though we do not experience energy on a physical level (with our physical senses), we can feel the energy as it shifts. The term often used to describe our complex relationship with the energetic plane is "emotion."

Our emotional state refers to the state of our energetic body, the body of energy that supports the physical body, as it changes in response to internal and external influences. Energy is in constant motion, and as the energy around us moves, so do we. In fact, the energy of our system (creation) is singular, one body of expressed motion giving rise to countless forms. States of energy are like waves in the ocean—one ocean, many waves. We interpret these states and assign them meaning—I am sad, I am angry, I am elated. And our intentions create energetic shifts that flow outward—I am angry; therefore, I act on my anger creating a wave of negative energy. Everything in creation as we know it is an expression of energy, just as energy is an expression of God.

The Spiritual Plane

God is eternally present as being and consciousness. Therefore, we could say that God occupies an eternal or ethereal plane of existence. Christian theologian, Paul Tillich, describes God as the "ground of being." Though I tend to refer to God simply as being itself, the ground of being is a useful description. As the ground of being, God occupies and is the spiritual plane within which all forms arise. The ground of being is the backdrop of creation, a space within which all things live and move and have their being.[8] The spiritual plane of existence is boundless. It is not a large expanse of

8. A reference to the Apostle Paul (Acts 17:28).

space, but a formless void.[9] We should not think of this ground as the absence of life, however, but as a boundless potentiality for life. God is both the space within which all forms arise[10] and the movement which propels them (AUM).

As human beings, we are human expressions of being itself. We are physical, we are energetic, and we are spiritual. The physical plane is an expression of the energetic plane, and both exist within the spiritual plane.[11] Energy rises from being and expresses itself physically. The spiritual plane does not change, just as spirit does not change. It simply is. The primary concern of spirituality is to open oneself to the presence of spirit. Though the spiritual plane exists eternally within and beyond us, we are rarely aware of it. Instead, we spend most of our lives focused on the constant movement of creation, energetic and physical. By opening ourselves to the presence of spirit, we open ourselves to possibility of living in peace—the eternal state of the spiritual plane.

The Mental Plane

Though we will discuss the mind's role in spirituality in the next chapter, it is important to note the existence and importance of the mental plane. The brain is a physical form comprised of innumerable neurons firing. We do not, however, experience neurons firing; we experience the results of neurons firing. We experience the movement of an arm, the opening of our eyes, and the beating of our heart. And we

---

9. Genesis 1:2 describes the earth, prior to creation, as "formless and void."

10. Kabbalah describes this space as *shekinah* (Hebrew: dwelling).

11. Again, there is no true division between these planes.

experience an entire universe of mental phenomena creating a plane of existence unique to each human.

The mental plane is a landscape of everchanging thought forms resulting in our unique perception of reality and identity. Reality is what we think it is, and we are who we think we are. We experience creation via the physical body, which is an expression of the energetic body. We have direct access to the world around us. Each experience, however, is interpreted and assigned meaning by the mind. We touch a tree. The signal from the tree activates neurons in the brain, and our experience of the tree is placed within a context of countless other experiences. We may have direct access to the tree, but we do not experience the tree in isolation.

We view life through the lens of the mind. Each experience is placed within the context of all experience. As we grow and change, so does our mental landscape. Thoughts are subtle forms. As the energy in my brain moves, neurons fire, and I experience forms rising within the mental plane. Most thought forms arising at any given moment are unconscious, meaning I am not aware of them. They are, however, integral components of the structure of my mind. They are part of my view of reality (perspective), and they are part of my view of myself (ego). I know the world directly through my participation in the energetic and physical planes. My understanding of these experiences, however, exists only in the mind.

THE FIRST FORM

In the beginning, when God moves as AUM, being becomes the first form. We have now moved beyond the eternal beginning, which is here and now, and into the inauguration of form within a system or plane of existence. If we could trace evolution back to the beginning of creation as we know it, we would discover a foundational element. The first form in a system creates the superstructure that will guide the system through its evolution. We exist within a system of energy, expanding toward more complex configurations of itself. All of creation is energy. AUM is the movement of God, the potential of all things to move. When AUM moves, it changes, becoming a singular expression of itself. In our reality, the first form is energy.

The movement of AUM creates an expression of itself and a plane of existence based upon the characteristics of the expression. Energy is the primordial element of our reality and the plane within which all subsequent forms exist. AUM moves as energy, and as energy moves it creates. Everything in the universe is an expression of energy moving. The moment AUM breaks the energetic plane, the evolution of creation begins. This is the beginning of creation as we experience it. It is not, however, the beginning of creation as we can measure it.

Many scientists refer to the beginning of the universe as the big bang. What they are referring to is the first appearance of potentially measurable phenomena, the moment energy is expressed as matter. Energy cannot be observed physically; therefore, it cannot be measured. But as soon as energy breaks the physical plane, we have a measurable phenomenon. Scientists are moving closer to understanding the nature of matter, from atoms to protons, neutrons and electrons to quarks and beyond. There are two concepts, however, that shape our view of reality, our understanding of creation, more than any other—space and time.

SPACE AND TIME

We see ourselves as occupying a certain area within a large expanse of space. In fact, we often refer to the area within which all stars and planets reside as "space." I am occupying an area of space, looking at a tree which occupies a separate area of space, within a more expansive area of space. All physical forms take up space. Space is the fabric of physical creation. Space is the physical plane. And it is a form in itself.

When energy breaks the physical plane, it expands outward as an ever-complexifying system of forms that we call the universe. The universe itself is comprised of countless physical elements; it is the physical plane (as far as we can tell). The universe is not emptiness. The universe is a physical form. As this form expands, so does the area within which all other physical forms reside. All physical forms occupy a section of space within the universe. The advent of the universe is the advent of space, and that space expands as the universe does.

I am here and you are there. This is space as we understand it, and this understanding regulates everything we are and do. But this is only half the story. We organize ourselves within space and time. Time, like space, is a tool of measurement. We utilize space to measure the orientation of physical objects within the physical plane. And we utilize time to measure their various rates of expansion. All forms expand as the movement of God (AUM) animates them. God moves as AUM, AUM expresses itself as energy, and energy expresses itself as matter. Life is movement; life is change. Time is the system we use to measure this change.

The concepts of space and time are valuable to our developing understanding of life. Space helps us to understand our physical location within the physical plane in reference to other physical forms. It helps us to orient ourselves within a larger system. Time helps us to understand temporality. All forms rise and fall, are born and die. Time helps us to embrace this simple truth. It also helps us schedule appointments and celebrate rites of passage. The important thing to remember is that space and time exist in relation to the expanding universe. They do not exist outside of creation. The advent of the physical plane is the advent of space and the beginning of the ticking clock we call time.[12]

COMPLEXIFICATION

Physical creation begins the moment energy breaks the physical plane as matter. This is also the advent of space and time as we understand them. Scientists are moving closer to uncovering the first physical expressions of energy—the first physical forms. Whether these forms are quarks or something even more fundamental, we can assume that they are exceedingly simple.[13] The first physical expressions of energy will be as close to actual energy as a physical form can be. Just as energy is the movement of God (AUM) actualized in our reality, the first physical form will be energy expressed as matter. As energy moves, matter moves. And as matter moves, life complexifies.

The beginning of the physical universe is a simple physical expression of energy. This inaugural element rises from the energetic plane and exists as the entirety of

12. Modern physics emphasizes the relativity of space and time or space-time. It is important to note that our concepts of space and time as tools of measurement are limited to our subjective experience.

13. For the purpose of our theology, I am presenting an overly simplified explanation of the origins of matter. A purely scientific approach would be much more nuanced (and beyond my capabilities).

physical creation. Once the form exhausts its resources, which is almost instantly with an exceedingly simple element, it falls back into being—expansion and contraction. Yet, as AUM moves eternally, energy expands, and a second physical element is created. This element is almost identical to the first. It is a simple expression of energy, save one slight variation. The second physical form is born into a reality that has already existed.

As the movement of God pushes life to expand, energy complexifies as variations of matter. The complexification of physical forms is based on two factors: the movement of God as energy pushing forms to expand and the interplay of forms within their environment. Life is movement, and life is change. Forms expand as they are moved by God and shift in relation to their environment. Life as we know it is the result of an ongoing evolution of forms interacting with one another as they are animated by God. Complexity is the natural result of movement and interaction.

New Seeds

A seed falls from a maple tree. This seed is the product of the parent tree and the result of millions of years of evolution. Encoded within the seed is a diagram for its growth. The parent tree has passed on this information as it was passed on by the tree that bore its seed, and so on and so forth. This new seed begins to grow; it begins to expand. This expansion is the result of energy, which is the movement of God expressed in creation. The seed expands from the inside out. It begins to express the patterns of movement that have been passed down to it from generations of trees. This seed, however, will not produce the exact same tree as its parent. The tree that grows from this seed will be unique.

First, the seed itself, though containing within it the genetic information of its parent, is a unique form from conception. The seed's growth is based on the unique environment of the parent tree and the environment that the parent tree exists within, which is slightly different from the environment of the "grandparent" tree. The seed will expand as the energy of life moves throw it, but its growth will be determined by the interaction of factors within the seed and without. Each seed will be slightly unique because of its orientation within the environment created by the parent tree.

Once the seed falls, it begins its life beyond the environment of the parent tree. The seed now exists within a natural habitat of shifting factors that will have a drastic effect on its growth. The seed cracks, and a tree begins to emerge. This tree will continue to expand in an ongoing interaction with its environment. Life is always moving and, therefore, always changing. As new forms arise, they do so in new environments. As these forms interact with a multitude of other forms, they evolve into new versions of themselves. Life expands as God moves within it. Life complexifies as each new form is born into a new environment. New seeds grow into new trees which produce new seeds.

ONWARD

The second physical form created by the movement of God as energy is born into an environment shaped by the first form. Thus, the second form will shift ever so slightly in relation to its new environment. Of course, the change will be virtually unnoticeable. The advent of the universe is comprised of forms so simple that their slight variations will be microscopic. But there is change, and that is all that life requires to begin its journey to you, me, and the vastness of creation.

The earliest forms in the universe expand and contract, continuously creating new life. Each form is born into an environment shaped by previous forms. As these forms expand and complexify, their breadth of existence grows. This means new forms are able to arise before existing forms die. Now forms can interact with one another which creates a whole new series of complexifications. We could, of course, go on and on, but a detailed description of evolution is not our intent. It is our intent to illustrate the existential relationship between a moving God and an ever-expanding universe.

The potential of being becoming is endless. As energy expands, forms interact and grow more complex, and the vast potentiality of energy inevitably comes to pass. Every combination of every form within every environment is only a matter of space and time. It is hard to imagine a simple expression of energy evolving into a complex human body, which is a hierarchy of innumerable forms in itself. But it has. You, the universe, and I were inevitable from the first divide.

Self-Actualization

And never say of anything, "I will definitely do this tomorrow," without adding, "if God so wills!"

—QURAN 18, 23—24[1]

WE MOVE AS GOD MOVES. God is both the silent witness of creation and the active principle pushing it to expand. Creation is the result of God's single desire to know itself. As God-the-subject witnesses God-the-object, God-the-object becomes so that it can be known. The movement of God-the-object (AUM) breaks the energetic and physical planes becoming the ever-expanding, ever-complexifying universe of forms we call "creation." But what role de we play in creation? Do we as human incarnations of being serve a specific purpose? Or are we just intelligent animals forever seeking meaning but never quite finding it? As God becomes all things, all things fulfill God's desire. We are God experiencing life. Our awareness of this simple truth changes everything.

---

1. Khattab, *Clear Quran*, 161.

KENOSIS

God creates in an act of self-emptying love (Greek: *kenosis*). For being to become, God as being must give of itself. God empties itself, pouring all that God is into creation. Being is boundless and, therefore, gives boundlessly. God does not choose what to create, nor does God limit itself in the creative act. God simply gives. The second chapter of Genesis states that God creates man by breathing into him.[2] This breath is the animating spirit of life (Hebrew: *ruah*). This is a powerful mythological image. It would, however, be more theologically accurate to state that God "moved in man" or "God poured itself into man."

Spirit (*ruah*) is the term we use to describe God's presence within life. But we must remember that spirit is God. We are animated by God, plain and simple. God is fully present within all of creation. God, as being, cannot be divided; being simply is. Each molecule within the universe contains as much of God as the universe itself. God is omnipresent: present everywhere in its fullness. God creates by emptying itself entirely, not because God chooses to, but because it is in God's nature to do so. The consequence of this outpouring is a creation that is forever expanding, forever complexifying, and existentially free.

CHOICE

Each moment is comprised of a vast hierarchy of forms acting and reacting. The way a form acts or reacts is determined by the hierarchy itself. As one form moves, all forms move. As one form acts, all forms react. Each form in the

---

2. The first human in Genesis is male, but, in creation, male and female have evolved together.

Self-Actualization

hierarchy is causally linked to every other. In the Hindu traditions, this phenomenon is referred to as *Indra's Web* or *Indra's Net*. *Indra*, king of the gods, spins the web of creation. At each intersection there is a jewel, a form, and reflected in each jewel is every other jewel. So, when one jewel changes, they all do. We are at the mercy of the hierarchy, influenced by countless internal and external factors beyond our control.[3] And, yet, we still choose.

Choice is the actualization of intention. When I make a choice, I think, speak, or move in the direction of a desired outcome, conscious or unconscious. The deterministic character of creation, sited above, is such that I can never fully grasp the factors that influence my intentions or their outcomes. I believe that I know why I choose, but the reality is I am only aware of a small portion of the influencers. It is not the impact of variables, however, that provides me with the ability to choose. It is my capacity for self-reflection.

A flower opens instinctively towards the sun. It does not make a choice; it simply responds. The lion chases the antelope. It does so as the result of evolutionary instinct. While the lion does have more agency than the flower, the lion does not have the capacity for self-reflection. We could say that the lion chooses to chase a particular antelope due to size or availability, but the lion is not reflectively aware of why it is doing so. As we witness the evolutionary journey from single-celled organisms to plants to primates to humans, we notice the subtle development of self-reflection.

Our capacity to choose has evolved as our self-awareness has evolved.[4] We cannot pinpoint the moment when the first of our species identified itself as an autonomous agent. But in crossing this threshold, we entered a new

---

3. A philosophical view called "determinism."
4. Self-reflection is the result of self-awareness.

plane of existence—mind. Rene Descartes is famous for the philosophical axiom, "I think, therefore I am" (Latin: *cogito, ergo sum*). This statement encompasses the totality of self-awareness. I cannot be sure of the validity of my thoughts, including my understanding of the world around me, but I know that I exist because it is I who am thinking this.

In a previous chapter, this "I" was identified with God, the single consciousness that is aware of all forms arising. Yet it is the evolution of the human mind that is responsible for self-awareness. We are aware that we exist (self-awareness), and we can reflect on the nature of this existence (self-reflection). We not only experience life as an expression of God; we know that we are experiencing life. We make choices based upon this knowledge.

Ego

Human beings have been evolving for hundreds of thousands of years. Sometime during our development, we awoke to the realization that each one of us is an autonomous agent, a unique form within a world of forms. The awareness of self can be conveyed by the axiom, "I exist." Each of us is a hierarchy of forms (atoms, molecules, compounds, etc.) within a larger hierarchy of forms (ecosystem, solar system, galaxy, etc.). But who is the autonomous agent? Where does the hierarchy end and I begin? The development of self-awareness coincides with the development of identity. Once I realize that I exist, I begin to question and subsequently define who I am. The human mind does not arbitrarily stumble upon a consistent definition of identity; it creates it.

As the mind evolved to reflect on the nature of existence, it began to separate certain aspects of creation dualistically. The primordial dualism is God and creation, subject and object. God is the one subject that is aware of all things (objects). This dualism, however, is an illusion. As all objects are expressions of God, all of creation is existentially one. But, to function as an autonomous agent, the mind must participate in the illusion.

As we experience life physically, the mind interprets these experiences as an interplay between distinct physical forms (physical plane). As we experience life energetically, the mind identifies energetic or emotional states of being (energetic plane). And as we experience life mentally, the mind organizes an entire altitude of mental phenomena into meaning, purpose, and, above all, identity. In the primordial dualism of subject/object, the subject becomes defined as the autonomous agent. I am the subject who is experiencing my life. God gets clothed in identity.

The mind views reality as a system of cause and effect within which it can participate. And the mind views itself as an autonomous agent that is both self-contained and responsible. Choice is the by-product of autonomy. I am able to choose because I have identified myself as an agent of choice. I believe that I am free because I believe that I can make choices. In fact, many would argue that freedom is the fundamental right of all humans. While freedom from external and internal bonds is a desirable and necessary pursuit, the truth is we rarely fully participate in the existential freedom of creation.

FREEDOM

God just gives. This is not God's choice; this is God's nature. Creation is the result of God's self-emptying. When God-the-subject witnesses God-the-object, God-the-object breaks the energetic and physical planes as form. Every form that being becomes, and the hierarchy of forms that we call "creation," is existentially free. God gives without coercion, without need, and without limitation. Every step in the evolution of the universe, the largest physical form we are aware of, has been the result of the interplay of forms within it. Life has not been planned. In fact, if it had been, life would not have meaning.

As I sit here typing, God's desire is actualized. God cannot experience typing without me. The purpose of life is to experience it. God becomes so that God can know itself as creation. Yet if my typing were preordained, the value of the experience would be nullified. The inherent meaning of each experience is embedded within the freedom to experience it. With each move of my finger across the keyboard, countless forms act and react freely creating a unique experience within the ever-shifting hierarchy of creation. It is the interaction of these forms that defines the nature of the experience, and it is the freedom of the forms to interact that makes the experience possible.

All forms act and react, but I am able to reflect on my circumstances and make choices based on desired outcomes. Who is this "I," and what control do I have over the actualization of my intentions? I can choose to type certain words. But the words that I "choose" are the result of numerous variables beyond the self-reflective mind. I think I know why I choose these words, but I can only grasp a small fraction of the variables contributing to the actualization of this moment. It is this grasping that defines choice.

Choice is an illusion created by the mind in its ongoing effort to sustain identity. In choosing, the mind seeks a limited outcome based upon limited variables. We move in the direction of these outcomes, oblivious to how little control we have over their actualization. Yet we choose, nonetheless. We continue to play into the mind's ongoing formation of identity and organize our lives accordingly.

God has no identity; God does not choose. Identity is the limited conception of self created by the mind, and choice is the movement toward limited outcomes based upon limited knowledge. God is unlimited and gives itself limitlessly in the creative act. It is creation that ultimately binds God. Each of us is a limited expression of the unlimited God. In order to realize our potential, we must let go of the illusion of control and allow God to move through us freely.

LETTING GO

We will never stop making choices; it is in our nature. As long as we have the capacity for self-reflection, we will strive to move in the direction of our intentions. Though duality is an illusion, it is an illusion that we must participate in. I see myself as an autonomous agent with the freedom to determine my own destiny. But what if I could see myself as both an autonomous agent and a collection of forms within the hierarchy? What if I understood intentionality to be essential while at the same time letting go of the need to achieve specific outcomes? What if I could fully participate in the unfolding of God as creation?

This moment is comprised of innumerable forms acting and reacting. Even if we could grasp the specific configuration of this particular frame of the hierarchy, it would shift immediately in an incomprehensible direction. Life is free, and freedom defies understanding. I do, however, have an awareness of my own specific circumstance. My mind continues to assimilate data gained from experience, physical and energetic, into its evolving conception of life and identity. This knowledge is not ultimate, but it is essential to my unfolding as a human expression of God's being.

Knowledge, Understanding, and Wisdom

Each and every experience adds an element of data to the mental plane. As my fingers touch these keys, the sensation adds a vital component to my knowledge base. I "know" what it is to type. And though I have touched these keys many times before, each experience is unique. Greek philosopher, Heraclitus, is famous for saying, "No man ever steps in the same river twice, for it's not the same river and he's not the same man." The river of life is constantly changing, and we are a part of that river. It is the interaction of human and river, of finger and keyboard, that provides the foundational elements of knowing. We know what life is because we experience it.

Knowledge and memory are closely linked. Each experience imprints a sensation on the mind. These sensations are added to the mind's vast storehouse of knowledge. Each sensation gained from experience is significant. Yet there is a phenomenon beyond knowing. With each experience the mental landscape shifts. The landscape is more than the sum of its parts. As we come to know life, we come to understand life. Our overall experience of life gives us a deep sense of what life is, of what life means. The more we know, the more we understand.

The mental landscape is a mosaic of countless individual experiences against a backdrop of evolutionary traits passed down from the experiences of our ancestors. While each individual picture in the mosaic is an element of our knowledge base, it is the picture in its entirety that represents our understanding of life and self. Life is what we understand it to be, and with each experience our understanding of life shifts. I am not the same person who struck these keys a moment ago. Each strike of the keyboard changes my understanding of life, even if subtly. As our knowledge base expands, our understanding deepens.

My perspective is unique. There is no one who has ever or will ever understand life the same way I do. This is the beauty of experience. I am God's agent in creation. As I see life, God sees life. Yet I will never understand God, nor will I ever fully understand life. My experience of God is not a tangible one. I experience God as being and consciousness, and these are unqualifiable. But I experience God nonetheless; and this experience, though incomprehensible, is accessible. It is the relationship between our experience of God and our understanding of life that creates wisdom.

Our understanding of life will always be limited, because our experience of life is limited. I can only know what I experience, and I can only understand what my experiences teach me. The experience of God, however, is unlimited because God is unlimited. I am experiencing the fathomless depths of God's being in every moment of my life. God is here and now, within these fingers, within these keys. Wisdom is the presence of God within our understanding of life.

Wisdom has a timeless feel to it. Whenever you hear something wise or speak wisdom, it feels as if you have accessed a timeless truth through the limitation of language and thought. Like revelation, wisdom is the outpouring of the absolute clothed in the particular. The breadth of our experience contributes to the depth of our understanding. The more we experience, the more we understand. But there is no depth of understanding that will guarantee our fulfillment. You cannot understand your way to peace. For this, you must be wise.

SELF-ACTUALIZATION

As God pours itself into creation, forms expand and interact producing increasingly complex configurations of life. A form, or collection of forms, is actualized when it reaches the full expression of its complexity. As the oak tree grows, it interacts with its environment. While the tree's genetic information is present within the seed, each oak tree will be unique. The amount of sunlight and rain that is available to the oak tree, even its placement in the soil and its proximity to other plants, will influence its potential. The actualization of the oak tree is dependent upon all these factors and more.

All forms are limited by their unique circumstances. And it is this uniqueness that defines a form's potential. Life is circumstantial. As we grow, the inner circumstances of our DNA, cells, etc., interact with the outer circumstances of our environment to create the inherent possibility for our lives. As noted earlier, most of these circumstances are beyond our control. While we can influence our circumstances through conscious action, we cannot change the overall framework of the reality within which we exist.

A young woman is born in an impoverished neighborhood in the inner city. Her father is a single parent who works two jobs in order to feed her and her two younger brothers. She works hard in school and at a part time job. Eventually, she is awarded a scholarship to attend a university. After four long years of growth and study, she ends up in a job that she loves and that pays her well. She continues to help her father and siblings, doing the very best that she can to ensure that they have every opportunity to prosper. Some would say that she took control of her life, changing the trajectory of the reality within which she was born. But she had much less control over her life than it appears.

She did not create her circumstances; she actualized them. Her intelligence and drive, the availability of part-time work, even the existence of a university to give her a scholarship—these were the circumstances that she had available to her, not to mention her ability to overcome any negative mental roadblocks that arise from being a child in poverty. No form has limitless potential, because creation itself is limited. It is not our duty to create something out of nothing. We have everything that we require. This does not mean that all circumstances are positive. There are those who are born into extremely negative circumstances. But they cannot create something out of nothing, and they do not have to.

Most forms will actualize their potential. The oak tree will grow as tall as it is able. Though a storm may tear it from the ground, the storm is a part of the tree's circumstances. Human beings are different. Though we are not existentially unique (all forms are expressions of being), we have developed a particular way of interacting with the environment. We have developed self-reflection, and this changes everything.

I was born within a unique set of circumstances like every form. As I grow and evolve, these circumstances change. Though the trajectory of my life is limited, I will encounter an array of possibilities with which to engage. And, most importantly, I am aware of some of these possibilities. It is this awareness that creates both the illusion of choice and the unique potential of the human condition. The oak tree is not aware of its environment. The lion is aware, but not self-reflectively aware. Self-awareness allows the human to examine its circumstances and reflect on how it should best proceed. And though most of the factors influencing the human are unknown, it is able to actively participate in its unfolding.

I cannot control the outcomes of my actions. I cannot change the reality within which I exist. And though I learn more about my circumstances every day, there are too many factors contributing to the trajectory of my life for me to predict what will happen next. Yet I am aware. I look around and I see the miracle of life unfolding. I am able to reflect on this miracle, and I am able to participate in God's desire. Life is beyond our control, but control is not the ultimate end.

AWAKENING

Each of us is born into a vast hierarchy of forms acting and reacting. We exist here and now, within a unique subset of creation. Our lives (mind, body, energy, and environment) are a completely unique expression of God's desire. Within this uniqueness lies the meaning of our lives and the path to our fulfillment. We do not exist to create a life that is not available to us. The purpose of life is to actualize our unique potential. To achieve this, we must get out of the way.

God is emptying itself into our lives here and now. We are the outpouring of God's unconditional love. The supreme goal of spirituality is to realize this and to participate in it. The illusion of control creates resistance to life, and resistance creates suffering.[5] We find peace when we let go of the illusion of control and accept what is. This does not

---

5. Buddha said that suffering is the result of selfish craving, which is related.

mean that we do not act; this does not mean that we do not strive to create change. It means that we act without attachment. According to Buddha, we aim the arrow, let it go, and *let it go*.

The oak tree will reach its potential, because its potential is inexorably linked to the potential of all of life. The potential of the human condition is unique as far as we can tell. Self-awareness has created the illusion of choice, and choice changes everything. We can reflect on reality and act in accordance with our own desires, fears, and beliefs. Or we can let go and fully participate in the unfolding of God through creation. God is moving through us here and now. The gift of humanity is to witness this.

In the End

If you would indeed behold the spirit of death, open your heart wide unto the body of life. For life and death are one, even as the river and the sea are one.

—KAHLIL GIBRAN[1]

EVERY STORY HAS AN ENDING. A cell, a molecule, a plant, an animal, or a star—each form rises from being itself, expands and complexifies, and, inevitably, falls back into being. Birth and death, beginning and ending, exist in a constant cycle that defines the very nature of existence. All things that are born must die. Without death, change would be impossible. And, without change, there is no creation.

EXPANSION

Life is movement, and movement is change. In the beginning, God divides and witnesses itself.[2] God-the-subject witnesses God-the-object, and God-the-object moves. This

1. Gibran, *Prophet,* 80.
2. Recall that the beginning is now.

movement is the one movement that makes life possible. As God moves, forms expand. As forms expand, they interact with other forms, and the hierarchy complexifies. With each shift in the hierarchy, *what was* comes to an end, and *what will be* is actualized. The birth of *what will be* depends on the death of *what was*. Beginning and ending are inexorably linked. As long as there is change, there will always be birth and death.

Every form within the hierarchy of creation is unique. Subsequently, the hierarchy itself is unique. As forms within the hierarchy shift, the hierarchy changes. This change moves the hierarchy from *what it was* to *what it will be*. Creation expands and complexifies because the forms within it expand and complexify. Thus, a new creation is constantly being born as the old creation dies. Life and death are in constant motion, happening at every level of creation. God's desire is to experience itself as life. And this desire pushes creation to become new in every moment.

Each form in creation is unique because of the qualities and attributes that define its character. Some forms are defined by physical qualities such as size and shape, some are defined by subtle qualities like the unique experience of each thought form, and some are defined by their relation to the constructs of time and space—the breadth of their existence and their relation to other forms in the hierarchy.[3] Each form comes into existence as an expression of God's movement and expands to meet its unique potential. It is this unique potential, defined by unique qualities and attributes, that makes each form finite.

Imagine air filling a balloon. The air moves into the balloon, pushing it to expand. As the balloon expands, it

3. For example, all electrons are identical but exist in various spaces with various quantum characteristics to help create unique forms of life.

takes on a specific shape. This shape represents the balloon's uniqueness and its limitation. It is the shape of the balloon that gives it character. Without shape, the balloon would have no boundaries and, subsequently, no defining qualities. However, once the balloon reaches its maximum size and shape, it cannot be filled anymore. The balloon is bound by the very qualities that make it unique. A balloon with no shape (no limitations) would have no characteristics. It would not and could not exist.

So it is with all forms. As God moves, a form expands. As a form expands, actualizes its uniqueness. The more a form grows, the more unique it becomes. The form expands and complexifies, along with the forms within it and beyond it, contributing to the ongoing evolution of life. And yet the form cannot expand forever. It is bound by the unique characteristics and attributes that define its character. Inevitably, a form must reach its full potential.[4] When this happens, the form is actualized, and God's desire is fulfilled.[5]

CONTRACTION

As God moves, forms expand. God is the animating principle of life, the one movement that moves all things. Like our breath, however, God does not only move in; God moves out. As God moves in, forms expand and complexify. Once a form, or hierarchy of forms, fulfills its unique potential as a created thing, God's desire is fulfilled. At this point

---

4. Recall that a form's potential is linked to the potential of other forms. When the potential of a tornado meets a young oak tree, the oak tree's potential will be affected.

5. Recall that time is illusion; thus, God's desire is always being fulfilled.

God moves out, and the form contracts. What was once animated by God's being is now void of life.

God is omnipresent, present within and beyond all things. God does not change. Forms expand to meet their unique potential and contract once that potential is met. We cannot measure God's movement. Even the term "movement" is symbolic. All that we know of God is mediated by our experience of creation. We say that God moves within us because we are moved by God. We say that God moves out because when we die, we are no longer animated by God's presence. "Movement" is analogous with life.

The earliest evidence for religious thinking can be found in the way our ancestors treated the dead. Mythologist Joseph Campbell asks us to imagine what our experience of death would be like at the dawn of self-reflection. This human being that I knew and loved is no longer here. The body is present, but something is missing; something has left. The physical matter is no longer animated by life. Our earliest musings about the reality of God emerged as we witnessed life and death.[6] God as the animating presence within and beyond all living things is the foundation of our spiritual experience and, subsequently, all religious thought.[7]

THE MOMENT

A moment can be defined as the experience of a particular configuration of forms within the hierarchy of creation.

---

6. See *Joseph Campbell and the Power of Myth*, Episode 3, "The First Storytellers."

7. *Animism* is the earliest form of religious thought and is characterized by the belief that all of life is animated by a transcendent reality or realities.

Each and every moment is unique because the configuration of forms can never and will never be repeated. A moment rises as forms shift from *what was* to *what is*. We experience the moment as sensory perceptions, emotional states (energetic states), and thoughts. We are human expressions of being experiencing a human perception of creation. We experience a moment rising, and then it is gone.

The nature of creation is such that we can never fully grasp the experience of being alive. We taste, touch, smell, hear, and see; we think and feel. Yet the forms that comprise these experiences are constantly shifting. Life cannot be held, and life cannot be stopped. It is natural that our minds seek to analyze the moment as it arises. As the hierarchy shifts, our minds sort experiential data adding information to their knowledge base and gaining a deeper understanding of life itself. But this understanding will always be limited, and just as the moment is being analyzed, it changes.

Trying to grasp the moment is like trying to hold the ocean in your hands. The ocean is far too immense for anyone to hold. And even the small fraction that we can grasp will seep from our hands immediately. The interaction of forms that make up each moment is greater still. We experience the moment as forms rising via the body and mind. Our experience is unique, it is temporary, and it is beyond our comprehension. But life is not meant to be held; it is meant to be experienced.

IN THE END

Each moment is unique. The forms around us and within us are constantly shifting. At every level of creation, life is beginning and ending. God-the-subject witnesses God-the-object becoming life here and now. We are a part of creation, an expression of God's desire to experience itself as life. With each moment that passes, creation becomes new; we become new. But, for this to happen, there must be death.

In the end, all things fade. Forms expand as they are animated by God's being and contract as God's desire is fulfilled. The mind that is thinking these thoughts, the fingers that are striking this keyboard, the trees outside my window—all of this will pass. We are not meant to hold on to life. We are meant to experience it. And we are meant to let it go. This is all that is asked of us by creation.

On Practice
An Epilogue to Creation

> *There is a community of the spirit.*
> *Join it, and feel the delight*
> *of walking in the noisy street,*
> *and being the noise.*
>
> —RUMI[1]

YOU ARE PARTICIPATING IN my primary spiritual practice, and for this I am grateful. In the Hindu traditions, this practice is called *Jñana Yoga* or the Yoga of Contemplation. In contemplating my experience of the divine, I am drawn to images that reflect that experience. These reflections draw me deeper into the presence of God creating a cycle of reception, creation, reception. I write theology because it is in the theological process that I feel most connected with God.

The image I like to use is that of a well. The living water[2] lies deep within the soil of creation—all we have to do

---

1. Barks, *Rumi*, 3.
2. In the *Torah*, the prophet Jeremiah refers to God as the living water.

is dig. We dig by engaging in activities that connect us with what I call God. For some, this is art or music. For others, it is religious ritual. Then, there are those who may find God in science and technology.[3] Yet, whatever our method of coming into conscious contact with the living water, it must be engaged with consistent effort. This is what makes spirituality a practice.

The living water is always available to us, deep within the fabric of creation. But the experience of life has a way of covering it up. We dig. Life adds dirt. We dig some more. It is not that life is trying to shield God from us. Remember, life IS God. Life is just distracting. We get pulled in by the ever-changing cacophony of sights and sounds and forget the space within which the noise echoes. Spiritual practice is the act of digging beneath the soil and accessing the source of all life. The more we dig, the more water we discover.

I cannot tell you what your spiritual practice should be. The religious traditions of the world provide tried and true methodologies for discovering God within creation, but these may not work for you. Where is the place you feel most connected to the world around you and yourself? What is the activity that brings you into harmony with the ground of your being? When do you feel most at peace, most loved? These are the questions of spirituality.

Spiritual practice should not be a side note. It should be central to your day-to-day process of living. We do not live so that we may dig; we dig so that we may live more fully. It is my hope and prayer that you find your way of uncovering the source of all things. And, in doing so, find yourself.

---

3. Some do not define their spiritual practice as "spiritual."

Bibliography

The Clear Quran. Translated by Dr. Mustafa Khattab. Illinois: Book of Signs Foundation, 2016.

The Essential Rumi. Translated by Coleman Barks. New York: Harper Collins, 2004.

"The Gospel of Thomas." In *The Gnostic Gospels of Jesus*, 7–25. Translated by Marvin Meyer. New York: Harper Collins, 2005.

Master Dogen's Shobogenzo. Translated by Gudo Nishijima and Chodo Cross. Tokyo: Dogen Sangha, 1994.

Campbell, Joseph, and Bill Moyers. *Power of Myth*. New York: Bantam Doubleday Dell, 1991.

Tolle, Eckhart. *The Power of Now*. Vancouver: Namaste, 1997.

Gibran, Kahlil. *The Prophet*. New York: Alfred A Knopf, 1923.

Aquinas, Thomas. *Selected Writings*. London: Penguin, 1998.

The Upanishads. Translated by Juan Mascaro. London: Penguin, 1965.

The Zohar. Translated by Daniel C. Matt. California: Stanford University Press, 2002.

www.ingramcontent.com/pod-product-compliance
Lightning Source LLC
Chambersburg PA
CBHW071746040426
42446CB00012B/2487